First published in 2007 by Conari Press,
an imprint of Red Wheel/Weiser, LLC
With offices at:
500 Third Street, Suite 230
San Francisco, CA 94107
www.redwheelweiser.com

ISBN: 978–1–57324–274–5
Library of Congress Cataloging-in-Publication Data available upon request

Cover and book design by Kristine Brogno
Typeset in Optima, Goudy, Handsome, and Earwig

Printed in Hong Kong
SS
10 9 8 7 6 5 4 3 2

How Old is BEAUTIFUL?

Marsha Karzmer

FOREWORD BY BJ GALLAGHER

Conari Press

FOREWORD

How old is beautiful? What a marvelous question! Beautiful is 16 . . . or 6 . . . or 46 . . . or 76. Beautiful is however old you are.

The colorful book you hold in your hands is remarkable for asking such a radical question. It is also remarkable in that is was "written" entirely by assembling bits and pieces from women's magazines — headlines from articles, phrases from ads, quips and quotes from sidebars. Marsha Karzmer takes the words of many women, from many sources, and assembles them in wonderful books. In a sense, then, these are the words of Everywoman.

And yet Marsha's own lyrical voice comes through crystal clear. Her sense of fun, her ability to find the humor in the mundane, and her zest

BJ GALLAGHER, author of *Everything I Need to Know I Learned from Other Women*

for life all animate the clips and quotes in this lovely book.

Conari designers have taken Marsha's "clip notes" and given them a look that can only be described as yummy eye candy! With its sumptuous colors, textures, graphics, and design, this lovely book is the perfect gift for girlfriends, sisters, moms, aunts, and any other important women in your life. This book tells them that they are beautiful . . . at every age!

You Must Remember This...

More than any antiaging regimen, a positive attitude will take years off your look

so

Celebrate the changes in your life!

aND

Balance your life
with the wisdom of

A Few
Good
Women

We are women and we can do anything!

WE MIGHT BE
WILD AND CRAZY

But Crazy in
A Good Way

WEIRD. BUT A GOOD KIND OF WEIRD.

Our mothers said we could have it all,

THEY ALSO SAID

"*Never go out of the house without your lipstick on.*"

So why do we apply mascara at 55 mph?
BECAUSE WE CAN.

We're living the possibilities our grandmothers only imagined— and some that exceed even their wildest dreams.

Oo, the possibilities!

IF YOU'RE A **REAL** WOMAN WITH **REAL** DREAMS THEN IT'S YOUR TURN TO START **LIVING LIFE TO ITS FULLEST!**

"You're never too old to reinvent yourself."

EVEN THE BEST CAN GET BETTER

It's you. Only better.

"*Just when the caterpillar thought the world was over,*

it became a butterfly." —ANONYMOUS

THE POWER OF

C H a N g E

Is In Your Hands

No, I don't have the same figure or face I had at 25, but hey, do I feel better about myself!

"I think every year I become happier because I become more confident and more comfortable in my own skin."

It's amazing how far a little attitude can take you.

In your mind you see a vision of yourself,

You're smart.
You're funny.
You're beautiful.
AT ANY AGE

"There's nothing more beautiful than a woman who embraces her maturity."

"With age comes the inner, the higher life. Who would be forever young, to dwell always in externals?"
— ELIZABETH CADY STANTON, SUFFRAGIST

"As we grow old…the beauty steals inward."

—RALPH WALDO EMERSON

believe in yourself

Hold on to Your Style

"I AM FREER
TODAY THAN I
HAVE EVER
BEEN—BECAUSE
I'M IN CONTROL.
FREEDOM TO ME
MEANS SELF-
KNOWLEDGE
AND SELF-
ACCEPTANCE."

"To love oneself is the beginning of a life-long romance."
—OSCAR WILDE

LOVE WHAT YOU'VE GOT —

WHAT A RADICAL CONCEPT!

Now that you've arrived,
ask yourself:
did you get there
by following
everyone else?

Why don't you LOVE YOURSELF just the way you are

Each year,
the hills get steeper,
the roads rockier,
the journey longer.

so

"I do more to take care of myself."

Here's some advice every
woman should take to heart:

When you push yourself to meet
a goal—whether it's running
a mile or a marathon—you develop
extraordinary confidence that
spills over into the rest of your life.

You
just know you can
handle anything that
comes your way.
And then you do.

Be inspired

Be open to new possibilities

DISCOVER THE SPONTANEOUS YOU!

For Crying Out Loud

You could be a woman dancing with abandon, throwing her head back and really laughing, raising her arms in victory after her first marathon.

No kidding!

Take Charge of Your Life!

STOP WORRYING
START DOING—

THERE ARE THOSE WHO DO.
AND THOSE WHO
WOULDACOULDASHOULDA.

Call Me Crazy, But I Have to Be Myself

Oh, I think I'm still very weird—I love working out, but I still have to talk myself into going to the gym every day.

I still kick butt.
(I just do it in more expensive shoes!)

A FEW YEARS AGO

"I looked at myself and thought, 'God, how did I get to be 47?'"

BUT

This is the
best time
in my life—

I like to think
of forty-plus
as the cocktail
hour of my
life. Now I'm
up for a really
good time!

OH, I WISH.

I knew
then what
I know now,

I DON'T KNOW

why women

THINK

IT'S ALL DOWNHILL AFTER 50

OPRAH TURNED 50!

And she is fabulous!

Why Don't More Women See Themselves:

as Young, Restless and Ageless

brilliant, fabulous

well-dressed.

"Women shouldn't compare themselves to other women. Men don't compare. Women are harder on themselves than men are."

Constant self-criticism eats away at self-esteem—and far too many women make a habit of it.

How successfully you age may have less to do with your genes or your lifestyle than with the way you see yourself in the world

**Just pick your
personal goal and**

GO FOR IT!

and

Eat Your Blueberries,
for Goodness Sake.

It's never too late…

To Treat Yourself Right.

WE'D LIKE
TO ENCOURAGE

You

**to push
the boundaries.**

What do women really want?

WE WANT

to feel in control. We want to feel strong, definitely strong. In our bodies and our minds.

STRONG
CAN BE
BEAUTIFUL

Here's to the
power of

STRONG
WOMEN

The Choice Is Yours

To find the answers
to life's minor and major
questions, listen to
your inner voice

Experience serenity.

Achieve balance.

Challenge yourself.

Wanna Feel Young Again?

DUST OFF YOUR DREAM AND MAKE IT COME TRUE

KICK UP YOUR *aura* AND SHOW YOUR **True Colors**

Unleash Your Inner

goddess

AND TRY

something new

WHAT'S YOUR IDEA OF FUN?

I KNOW YOU LIKE TO SHOP TILL YOU DROP

*Nice try, honey,
but it's not enough.*

Every mind has the ability to dream great dreams.
Every person on this planet, no matter how big or
small, is filled with potential. Every idea, no matter
who or where it comes from, is full of possibilities.

It's not how many ideas you have.
It's how many you make happen.

DREAMS DO COME TRUE.

**Yes, Real Women
Like You
Can Achieve
Unreal Success**

"Each day comes bearing its own gifts. Untie the ribbons."

*the beauty and
mystery of this life
is not in arriving at
answers, but in the
process of seeking.*

"I FEEL BLESSED FOR THE GOOD EXPERIENCES IN MY LIFE, AND

ALSO FOR THE BAD ONES. I'VE LEARNED A LOT FROM BOTH."

Life is a roller coaster. **But** some days when you wake up in the morning, everything just feels right. those are the days we live for.

Beauty is what happens
when you're busy living life.

"Beyond living and dreaming
there is something more important:
waking up." —ANTONIO MACHADO

> "I now realize that each new day is a gift that should be appreciated."

EVERY DAY ABOVE GROUND IS A GOOD ONE

Just to be alive is a grand thing.

THIS WAKING UP THING IS NOT SO BAD AFTER ALL.

If you
want to

FEEL YOUNG AGAIN.

Live more. Yawn less.

You Gotta Have Adventures

You must pray that the way be long,
full of adventures and experiences.

at every age

Remember.
It's not just
where you
go in life.
It's how you
get there.

Life is a journey.

Give your life story
some exclamation points.

There are mountains to
climb, oceans to swim,
Ferris wheels to ferris.

"The trick is to grow up without getting old."

—FRANK LLOYD WRIGHT

"Live your life and forget your age."

The Only Person You Need To Be
IS YOURSELF.

**You're on the threshold of
a whole new life.**

**The
image we
have of
ourselves
IS ALL THAT MATTERS**

JUST Say "Old and Lousy"

is not in my vocabulary!

NOT NOW. NOT EVER.

I WAS BORN WRINKLED.

I WILL DIE WRINKLED.

BUT I LIKE ME.

*How much do you need
to see to know I'm beautiful?*

real **beauty** comes from within

Let the world **SEE** you the way you see **YOURSELF**.

It's what's inside that counts.

You'll only get better with age...

Inner strength means outer beauty.

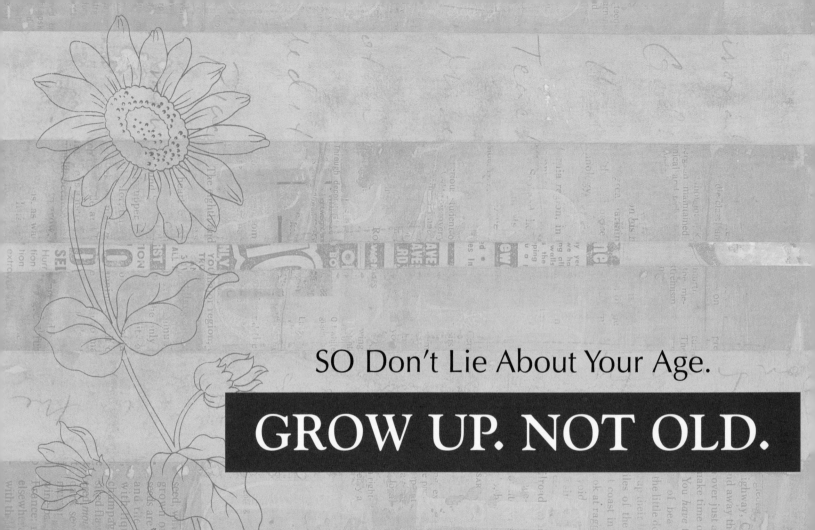

SO Don't Lie About Your Age.

GROW UP. NOT OLD.

"There is no old age.
There is, as there always was,
just you."

—CAROL MATTHAU, WRITER

Live Your Best Life

THE MOST IMPORTANT ACT IS ALWAYS

THE DESIRE TO STAY UNIQUE.

Judge me on looks?

You're just scratching the surface.

Love Me, Love My Imperfections

I am peaceful and strong.

AND NOW, THE TRUTH.
WE KNOW WE CAN'T STAY

Forever Young

But

There's no reason
not to be cool!

REALLY COOL

*thank God
you're a woman!*

A WOMAN.

CREATIVE, MYSTICAL
INTUITIVE, AND
MAGICAL

Oops, we left something out.

IN OUR TWENTIES AND THIRTIES, WE
DREAMED BIG DREAMS AND MADE
LONG-RANGE PLANS. AFTER 40, WE
HAVE TO ASK: WHAT MAKES US
HAPPY TODAY?

"People are just about as happy as they make up their minds to be." ⬛ Wake up happy—even on Monday morning!

if we are truly happy inside, then age brings with it a maturity, a depth, and a power that only magnifies our radiance.

My Secret For Happiness

is LIVING MOMENT TO
MOMENT, AND APPRECIATING
THE MOMENTS THAT
I DO HAVE.

We do not remember days we remember moments.

It is said, life gets better one moment at a time.

and

**Whatever you do,
don't forget the heart.**

IF YOU HAVE HEART,
AGE DOESN'T MATTER.

It turns out the secret to

HAPPINESS
at Every Age
IS

Love

love — A MUST-HAVE
FOR EVERY AGE

I LOVE LOVE

AND

I love life

The Rumors Are True!

IF YOU LOVE

you

LOOK YOUNGER

SO LET'S HAVE

A toast to love and laughter and

happiness ever after. WHAT IT COMES DOWN TO IS

the first **80** years are definitely the hardest.

aND

EVERYONE LOVES
a great finish.

beauty has no age limit.

ACKNOWLEDGMENTS

Many thanks to fellow writer BJ Gallagher for her early encouragement and enthusiastic support.

Thanks to Jan Johnson and Brenda Knight at Conari Press for seeing my
"clip notes" vision and bringing that vision into reality as this beautiful book.

Thanks to Jason Bostocky for letting me make all those color copies of my early "ransom books."

Deep thanks to my amazing kids — Jonah, Justin, Carly, and Jordan. I'll love you for always.

Most of all, love and appreciation to my husband Dave for teaching me to never give up.

*Dedicated to the memory of
my mom and dad.*

To Our Readers

Conari Press, an imprint of Red Wheel/Weiser, publishes books on topics ranging from spirituality, personal growth, and relationships to women's issues, parenting, and social issues. Our mission is to publish quality books that will make a difference in people's lives—how we feel about ourselves and how we relate to one another. We value integrity, compassion, and receptivity, both in the books we publish and in the way we do business.

Our readers are our most important resource, and we value your input, suggestions, and ideas about what you would like to see published. Please feel free to contact us, to request our latest book catalog, or to be added to our mailing list.

Conari Press
An imprint of Red Wheel/Weiser, LLC
500 Third Street, Suite 230
San Francisco, CA 94107
www.redwheelweiser.com